INNER BUTTERFLIES

NICOLETTE L. TOTH

authorHOUSE®

AuthorHouse™
1663 Liberty Drive
Bloomington, IN 47403
www.authorhouse.com
Phone: 1 (800) 839-8640

Published by AuthorHouse 08/20/2019

ISBN: 978-1-7283-2254-4 (sc)
ISBN: 978-1-7283-2252-0 (hc)
ISBN: 978-1-7283-2253-7 (e)

Library of Congress Control Number: 2019911477

Print information available on the last page.

Any people depicted in stock imagery provided by Getty Images are models,
and such images are being used for illustrative purposes only.
Certain stock imagery © Getty Images.

This book is printed on acid-free paper.

Because of the dynamic nature of the Internet, any web addresses or links contained in
this book may have changed since publication and may no longer be valid. The views
expressed in this work are solely those of the author and do not necessarily reflect the
views of the publisher, and the publisher hereby disclaims any responsibility for them.

Contents

The Savory 45

The Sour

he's evil

his lips are sour
and his spiky hair
made from knifes
that cut deep into her soul
and he left his mark

color blind

i saw everything
the red in your eyes
and the blue in your lips
you never caught a glimpse of what
i showed you
the gold in my eyes
and the pink in my smile
that could easily get lost
inside the darkness
you decided to show,
i still chose you
and with that
being the worst mistake
my smile then was no longer pink
but black
and my golden eyes
were now grey
because of the absence of color
which i got lost in,
lost in you

under water

trust me

trust me

trust me

she murmurs under her breath

as the shiver

of darkness

crawls across her body

and her hazy eyes

start to water

she tries to speak

but finds no breath

and she's left feeling alone

once again

ninety-three million miles

sitting right next to me
and all i can think about
is how your part of my solar system
your the fire
on the sun
water
to the earth
yet i feel like you are
ninety-three million miles away

closed hearted

you can pretend you don't care
you can pretend you don't cry
over the things you spill
into my open heart
but once my heart isn't open
you won't be able to pretend anymore

self-sabotage

put on a show to entertain
step out of character
and you feel your pain
that was there anyway

never

someone's going to care
for me
cause you never do

and he'll show my inner butterflies
how to fly out again
cause you never did

guilty for me

i am as fragile
as glass
and you not only
broke me
but tried to
put me back
together
with your bleeding hands
and felt the pain
i had to feel

happy

bullets
you fired at me
struck
just how you wanted them
right through
my heart
and it gave me a sense
of lust
i thought i wanted
it wasn't
after i saw right through your intentions
which wasn't to bring me
"happy"
but to kill *a part of me*
from ever seeing it again

silence

i lay in a bed
full of petals taken from roses
what you see is the delicacy of them
what you don't
is what is **hidden**
the thorns behind my back
picking every nerve it could reach
the pain
unimaginable
i cover my emotions with the sheets
but
screaming inside
though you only hear silence
i'm chocking on my own words
yet you still only see my silhouette
a silhouette hiding scars from thorns
but i choose to only show you the beauty; which i portray

not your everyday fairytale

sweet boy
can i ask what's wrong
why you say you are living your *worst nightmare*
can i ask why you're in so much pain

sweet girl
i wish i could say
I wish i could
but you are the main character
in *my worst nightmare*

cycle of love

create then destroy

crazy romantics

rose petals
and champagne
the romantic moonlight
shining into the candle lit room.
you believe there
to be a story about love,
at where the story ends.
when really it is a "love story"
of two hearts
so in love
in causes
pain
and by the end of this story
the tub is not filled
with bliss and joy
but the dangerous amount of "love"
turn into revenge and hate.

cry me an ocean

i swam through oceans for you
you didn't know
you made me *cry those oceans*

you were the storm

sound of raindrops
remind me of how i used to feel
after you were gone

and not because you left
but because i stayed

and i thought you were the sun
but really you were the storm

it still smelled like you

i scream and yell
every night
into that same pillow
we both used to sleep on
"it still smells like you"
i think to myself every night
every dream
i dream
you haunt
and haunt
until i end up waking;
it started with just a few tears
but every night
the more dreams
i dream
and the more you haunt
and haunt me
the more tears fell from my dewey face
and yet still
even thought my pillow was soaked
"it still smelled like you"

reality hits hard

the rain starts pouring, everything is fine
until you see the lightning
then hear the thunder
it's all unexpected
and happens by chance
chance that
sends a shock throughout one's body
your heart sinks
and your face seems to turn to snow
now this
ask yourself
is this real
and close your eyes
and clench them harder
to open them
to the same reality you were in before
the lightning
and the thunder
seem to fade
as you do too

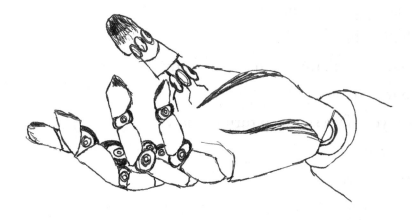

controller, control her

your face is a statue
that was constructed
to remind me of how much i miss you
and how even when i think of you
i feel your energy in my room

i tear up when i remember what
hell you dragged me through

but the saddest part
is that i was by your side

and no
i never realized until now
that you were using me

it had felt like it was real

i know never to talk to you again
or you'll do the same

but that's all i ever wanna do

i can't live without you

how could you leave me?
without your energy

you left me dead
as if the sun were to explode
as if you took away the oxygen i need
to breathe

you took it away
like a rose
without water
sun
air
soil
i could instantly feel
how cold it got inside

all because
you left me without your energy

but, i forgive you

when i felt nothing inside me
and no one around me
i thought you filled my void

and helped me get through
the depression
that rained on my shoulders
everywhere i went

a cloud that just got heavier
and heavier
i tried to stop it from raining
it just made it pour
and not just from the cloud

but from my sad eyes
and weary mouth
and still you have only filled that void
with honey, not love

i'm a rose, with no thorns

how would you feel
if i took away
your air
your sun
and your water

you'd be dead
like me
a rose

who had no thorns

The Savory

fire and ice

they were fire and ice
he bought the heat
and left her cold
until she found someone better
and let him burn
then she blew out his flame

honey, not love

honey; sugar sweet,
the taste of his lips
can make you *bleed*
with passion
with a feeling
of "safe"

honey; sugar sweet
taste of her lips
turn your veins
to honey,
sugar
sweet.

glass flowers

my emotions; broken glass
my tears; liquid fire

a glass flower broken by *lightning*
the sun behind the clouds
lightning
thunder
rain
all happening at once
sunshine
glass
a flower
but never again the same

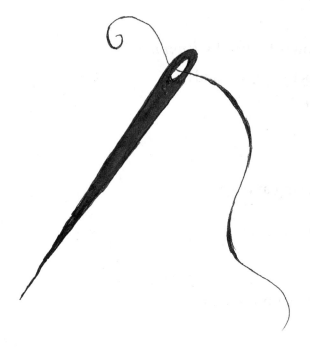

threads

"she is hanging by a thread"
a thread that comes from
the unbalanced life
she has lived through
this is **her**
thick skin
she has built
to keep herself
alive.

somethings gotta change

i thought i could handle it
but honestly
i can't
according to your
judgmental head
full of voices
that can't lay to rest
i thought i could handle it
i put all my feelings into bottles
that ended up spilling
and getting me in
trouble
i thought i could handle it
be the only one
here for it
now i have to handle
all of my restlessness
still i think i can clean
up my mess

but really
i'm all in my head
and speaking to all
your voices
that can't lay to rest
still think
i
could handle
it.

who will?

if you won't save me from myself
who will?

street sign

what do i do next

the street sign is telling me to go left

i listen

and next, i really can't seem to catch my breath

i'm okay

to love someone
may be a blessing
but what is it about them
that they make you keep on missing

i'm okay
isn't something
you'll end up say

what is it about them
that brings you to your knees
and not your feet

count your blessings
but learn your lessons

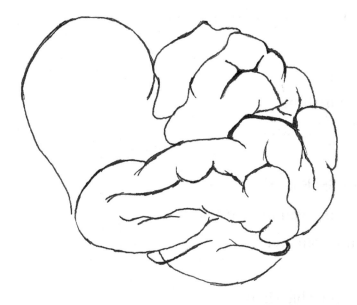

love or logic

can i ask
what is it we
really
had
thinking with our heart
and "loving" with our minds
if this is what love is i doubt
you will ever find it again

you

wake up
look in the mirror
to
see a stranger
starring into your eyes
but it's better than the old you
the pain that it bought is now gone
you had to get rid of the mask
and finally burn it

jealous

love is *endless*
and infectious
love;
restless
and out of all people
it made you jealous

you and i are like tears

chasing each other
one obstacle
after another
once we have fallen
we just pull each other down
and
we are now falling
together

i'm human

tears are just emotions we can't express

yes, no, yes

being confused isn't simple
there isn't just a left and right
there is one hundred million in-betweens

confused

you confuse me
i can never put a finger
on what your feeling
not even bob ross
could paint the picture you
want me to receive.

stop giving the world to the people who don't deserve it

here is my heart
here is all i own
here is everything i can give

is that not enough?

that's okay let me give you more

no angel

she might love to watch the stars
listen to classics
and look like an angel
buts she's no angel

a creation

the paintbrush
brittle
and covered in
coats of colors
can create a
piece of art
portraying the artists
feelings
and ricochet
not only through
and to the canvas,
but to the twisted
and complex minds
of other
broken souls.

The Sweet

she's beautiful

she has sweet lips
and an intimidating stare
she struck like lighting
and forever scared his heart

universe

you found a place for me
even if i didn't know i had one

thank you

:))))

if it's cliché
i don't wanna hear it
but i love you

snow white

give me the apple
i'll take a bite
you're my poison
there's none in sight
i can't make the mistake
like snow white

welcome home

seeing your reflection
doesn't mean you think anything is possible
because of where you have come from
but believing in yourself
is

angels

in the eyes of an angel a love-song
a heartbeat
and the tears we cry
nothing else matters
then what is behind the mask
the beauty and love
in the smallest corners
of our body

what is in the mind
the eyes
and the emotions
is the skin
that should be shown

dreamy

sing me a lullaby
and when i fall asleep
the only thing i'll be dreaming of is you

once i wake up
there you are next to me
better than anything i could of dreamed of

displaying her

her aura shines as if it were made of crystals

her hair

beautiful and blonde

her subtle laugh

makes everyone go crazy for her

her imperfect

perfect body

that has been through so damn much

i have fallen in love with her

a body

my body

call me a princess

hoodies are my crown

no lipstick just

mansions as my castle

i call my friends

royalty

but still

you can call me a princess

blue and yellow roses

you said your favorite color was yellow
i see the sun and think of you
i see the sunflower painted on my wall
and imagine us together
i see yellow everywhere now
and the only thing i can think of
is "i wonder if he's thinking of me,
when i told him
he was my favorite
shade of blue"
his aura can strike you from
100 miles away
and his tears
which he "never" cries;
are the perfect shade of blue
do you think of me when you look at the day light sky
or when you stare into the moonlight
there's only one way to find out
if i'm your favorite shade of yellow

i see you the next day
holding green roses
you hand them to me and say
"you are the perfect shade of blue to my yellow,
green"

huh

i'll be your villain
in a story
just so you'll keep chasing me

still falling

i guess I'm falling with you
and deeply
into a place no one knows how to explain
no matter how far the fall
i won't try and stop myself
it's like falling in a dream
except you don't hit the ground
in real life

the air inside my lungs
are now only filled
with yours
and with you on my side
still falling

i don't think i'd ever wanna hit the ground
at-least not without you

my romeo do you dream of me?-juliet

crazy how your hair can make me
swim through oceans
how your eyes allow me to get lost inside you
how your perfect face
confuses me in what
direction to follow
in the maze
you placed me in
and even your laugh can easily put me in a daydream
only i create within

do you ever get lost in my sunset colored eyes?
do you ever wanna surf over my shiny blonde hair?
am I ever in your
daydream?

clear skies

rainbows are the skies smile
after a rainy day

i love you

who knew you would come into my life
and at the perfect moment
without hesitation
you said
yes
if it made me happy
without hesitation
giving me the world
you thought was never enough
so, you brought
the sun and stars
and still you think it didn't make me happy
as if that wasn't enough
you brought me
even the moon
and every single planet out there

i wish you knew now
what i really wanted

you

inner butterflies

she took a breath in
she took a breath out
her heart filled with light
and her
smile
lit up.

her aura glowed
and reached his
he took a breath in
he took a breath out
his inner butterflies
fluttered into her light

they took each other's
breath away
first in
then out
as their inner butterflies
fluttered into
each other's life.

Nicolette has always been able to channel her deep emotions, and being a teenager there is a lot to write about, so that's what she did. But she didn't just want to share her feelings with a notebook or a computer screen. Writing to have a purpose is what she cared about, and to allow readers to get lost in her thoughts.

Printed in the United States
By Bookmasters